CW00590028

LIVING STREAM MINISTRY

Character

WITNESS LEE

Living Stream Ministry

Anaheim, California • www.lsm.org

First Edition, August 1987.

ISBN 978-0-87083-322-9

Published by

Living Stream Ministry
2431 W. La Palma Ave., Anaheim, CA 92804 U.S.A.
P. O. Box 2121, Anaheim, CA 92814 U.S.A.

Printed and bound by CPI Group (UK) Ltd, Croydon, CR0 4YY

09 10 11 12 13 14 / 14 13 12 11 10 9 8

CONTENTS

PREFACE

The messages contained in this book were given between 1953 and 1968 in two locations, Manila, the Philippines, and Taipei, Taiwan. They have been translated from the Chinese.

Chapter One

CHARACTER

THE FIRST GROUP—GENUINE, EXACT, STRICT

1. Genuine

The opposite of genuine is false. He who pretends is not genuine. Genuineness forms one's foundation and base. A person who is not genuine is baseless and cannot be entrusted with great responsibilities. Genuineness in character is the ability to sacrifice for others. Merely to be an honest person is not sufficient; one must be genuine. One who is not genuine may be welcomed by others initially, but the welcome will not last. Over time, it is genuineness which gains people's hearts. To inspire others' confidence, one must possess a genuine character.

2. Exact

Most people are loose; few are truly exact. One who is punctual does not procrastinate. One who is accurate in his words is dependable, and one who is precise in his work is trustworthy. Rare and precious is a person who is perfectly accurate.

3. Strict

Genuineness and tightness make up exactness, which in turn is manifested in strictness. Looseness leads to inaccuracy; he who is exact is always strict. The secret to a punctual person is his strictness. Only by being strict can one be genuine and exact.

THE SECOND GROUP—DILIGENT, BROAD, FINE

1. Diligent

Few people are diligent; most prefer leisure to labor. Once a person becomes lazy, he can accomplish nothing. Romans

12:11 says, "Not slothful in zeal," and Proverbs 6:6 says, "Go to the ant, thou sluggard; consider her ways, and be wise." Why do laziness, gluttony, and sleep go together (Titus 1:12)? It is because all lazy people pity and love themselves, and thus naturally love to eat and sleep. However, 2 Thessalonians 3:10 says, "If anyone does not want to work, neither let him eat."

All four points mentioned above are related to dealing severely with oneself.

2. Broad

It is easy for one who possesses the foregoing character traits to become narrow. He must therefore pay attention to having a "broad" character. The Chinese language uses an expression meaning "ocean" to illustrate a person's capacity to be as large as the ocean. "And God gave Solomon...largeness of heart, even as the sand that is on the sea shore" (1 Kings 4:29). Since sand encompasses the sea, the biblical requirement concerning broadness is greater than that conveyed by the Chinese expression. The impact of a person's life-work has much to do with his being either broad or small. A petty person can never accomplish great things.

3. Fine

A person with a broad capacity often fails to be fine, leading to negligence and inevitable loss. One ought to be broad but not rough, fine but not small.

THE THIRD GROUP—STABLE, PATIENT, DEEP

1. Stable

To be stable is to be solid and not easily moved, not panicky, hasty, or anxious. Stability, however, differs from slowness. Being slow means not acting when there is time to act, while being stable means allowing time to do its work. A stable person does not make decisions lightly or carelessly, nor does he easily praise or condemn others. When a situation is not entirely clear to him, he stops and does not speak or express his opinions carelessly. Neither does he proceed casually in matters that are serious, uncertain, or

incomprehensible. Paul, a stable person, said to the Corinthians, "Our word toward you is not yes and no" (2 Cor. 1:18).

2. Patient

Patience here does not refer to endurance but to the ability to wait, as mentioned in James 5:7, "The farmer awaits the precious fruit of the earth." Patience differs from slowness. To be slow is to miss a present opportunity, whereas to be patient is to anticipate a coming opportunity. One should not be slow, but one should be able to wait, working diligently without ever losing hope. Merely to hope, however, is vain; one should trust in his own ability to accomplish things. A patient person is able to remain still when he is in pain. The farmer who patiently awaits his harvest from the earth is allowing time to do its work. Patience is not passivity; it is aggressiveness without anxiety.

3. Deep

To be deep is to be not shallow or superficial. It is to base one's judgment on evidence rather than appearance. It is neither to be nagging nor to be bothersome, but simply to be serious. In any case, one should be deep but not overly inquisitive, since a prying person is useless.

THE FOURTH GROUP—PURE, JUST, CALM

1. Pure

To be pure and unadulterated is a matter of motive, of being free of ulterior intentions.

Deuteronomy 22:9 says, "Thou shalt not sow thy vineyard with divers seeds: lest the fruit of thy seed which thou hast sown, and the fruit of thy vineyard, be defiled." God is never pleased with men doing a mixed work. In the end, ulterior motives always create problems.

2. Just

To be just means to be unbiased, to handle all matters fairly. For example, it is to be judicious in one's evaluation of others. Faults invariably exist among the good, and merit among faults. To be just, one must be impartial, paying equal attention to each aspect of a person or matter, appraising it from different angles and putting it in its proper place.

This is not a matter of spirituality or morality but of character. Both the teacher who expounds the Scriptures and the elder who administrates the church must possess a just character. One cannot do anything rightly if there is the element of injustice in his character. To illustrate, an inaccurate level can never produce an even surface.

3. Calm

The human heart is usually tempestuous. In dealing with important matters, a person who serves the Lord must remain calm in his mind, emotion, and will. One who is not calm cannot resist incitement and external influence. The way to practice calmness is by (1) not acting quickly and (2) not believing rumors, which inevitably cause agitation.

THE FIFTH GROUP—SINGLE, CORPORATE, OPEN

1. Single

To be single and unscattered is related to being pure, just, and calm. A person should either not undertake a task at all or do it single-mindedly. He must be single, whether he is studying, managing a home, or doing business. Singleness brings about concentration, which in turn produces positive results. A person who is not single-minded can never perform a task well.

2. Corporate

To be corporate is to be not individualistic, selfish, or reclusive. Singleness in character must be balanced by a corporate quality.

3. Open

An open believer is able to receive spiritual help. He who is the most open receives the most help and can be the most helpful. How important is an open character among believers!

However, this must not be a natural and unrestrained open-ness but one that, like doors and windows, can be opened or closed readily.

Matters that are absolutely personal, private, and unrelated to others need not be disclosed. The disclosure of one's private affairs never benefits either the teller or the hearer. It is un-necessary to be open concerning matters in which one does not need help or cannot offer help, since such openness is futile.

THE SIXTH GROUP—
AFFECTIONATE, ARDENT, ACCOMMODATING

1. Affectionate

Affection implies both nearness and love. In particular, it stresses care, sympathy, and intimacy. A person without an intimate concern for others cannot bring others to salvation through the gospel. Neither can such a person be a responsi-ble one in the church.

2. Ardent

Being ardent goes beyond being affectionate. Whereas affection is in the heart, ardor implies outward action which resolutely brings others to salvation and helps them to reach the goal. Ardor is fervent and powerful.

3. Accommodating

Herein is the principle of incarnation. If God had not come into the world through incarnation to accommodate Himself to men, but had merely loved men and desired that they return to Him, He could not have accomplished redemption. One must reach out to others in order to lead them to salva-tion. Only those who fit in with people are able to preach the gospel to them in order to save them. Unless one can accom-modate himself to those who are younger and lowlier, he will find it difficult to lead them.

THE SEVENTH GROUP—STRONG, PLIANT, SUBMISSIVE

1. Strong

Strength denotes firmness, not hardness. One ought to be

strong but not hard, that is, strong in will but not hard in heart. The Apostle Paul said, "Be a man, be strong" (1 Cor. 16:13).

2. Pliant

Strength must be matched by pliancy. The expression in Chinese is "to temper strength with pliancy." Strength without pliancy is hardness, which inevitably spoils things, whereas pliancy without strength results in softness, which also is useless. A watchband is both firm and flexible, capable of being bent or stretched at will.

3. Submissive

To be submissive is to be obedient and yielding. Some can only teach people to follow orders, but they can never submit to others. One should realize that the person who can best give orders is the person who can best receive them. Submission is an element of the divine life. Those who possess this life do not consider it shameful but proper to submit and to take orders.

The one who gives orders bears a heavy responsibility; those who take them bear none. How blessed it is to listen to others and to be covered in everything.

THE EIGHTH GROUP—SUFFERING, LOWLY, POOR

1. Suffering

Suffering works endless wonders. There are some things which one cannot pass through without suffering. The more a person is able to suffer, the more useful he is. One who is not ready to suffer cannot accomplish great things. Fitting is the ancient proverb, "He who endures the worst of sufferings is the best among men."

2. Lowly

One should aim high but conduct himself in a lowly way. Romans 12:16 says that we should be "led away to the lowly." Only by taking a lowly position can one help others. No matter how respected and highly esteemed a person may be, he should take a lowly position. This is not to pretend to be humble but rather to genuinely confess from the heart that one has nothing of which to boast.

First Peter 5:5 says, "God resists the proud, but gives grace to the humble."

3. Poor

The world covets position and riches, but a Christian must be content with and even choose poverty. Poverty has its usefulness as well as its delight. However, one should not make himself poor by being lazy. Such poverty is worthless and futile. A willingness to be poor for the Lord's sake when one has the ability and even the opportunity to be rich, or a practice of spending all one's money for the Lord, are both rare and precious. The life of Christ is a life that chooses to be poor. Consider how He left His throne to be born in a manger and to live in Nazareth, tasting all the privation of human life.

THE NINTH GROUP—STEADFAST, ENDURING, BEARING

1. Steadfast

Steadfast means persevering. The best is usually reserved for last. Anything that grows quickly also withers quickly. Nothing that is deep, weighty, and superior can be obtained in a short time or by chance. Specifically, there are no shortcuts in spiritual things. Steadfastness and perseverance are the prerequisites for gaining that which is excellent.

Many Bible truths which are at first incomprehensible despite one's desire to know them eventually become understandable through persistent reading of the Scriptures. To be steadfast is to not covet the grand and quick results. There is an old saying that "drops of water eventually can penetrate a stone."

2. Enduring

One who is able to endure is able to withstand mistreatment. Do not mistreat others, but endure their mistreatment. A young man should not avoid ill-treatment and take the easy way out; rather, he should suffer abuse willingly. The more difficult the lesson, the deeper and more profitable it is.

3. Bearing

A person of character must be able to bear pressure. Anything that is solid and strong must first be pressed. A diamond is formed through intense pressure. That which grows without restriction usually is not beautiful. However, do not invite others to put pressure on you; rather, you should put yourself under pressure. The combination of the five preceding character traits—suffering, lowly, poor, steadfast, and enduring—gives a person the ability to bear pressure.

THE TENTH GROUP—CLEAR, MAGNANIMOUS, GRAVE

1. Clear

Clarity here does not mean brightness; it denotes understanding. People are often ignorant of their own dullness and stupidity. One should know himself as well as others.

2. Magnanimous

Being magnanimous is similar to being broad. To be broad is to be tolerant of others, and to be magnanimous is to be not cruel to others. In dealing with others, one must supplement affection, ardor, and accommodation with magnanimity. It is difficult to have an enemy-loving life without a magnanimous character. A cruel person is always jealous, while a magnanimous person is able to forgive. It is permissible to speak severely to others, but never cruelly. Neither should one be foolishly kind.

3. Grave

One who is grave is not frivolous. Whatever a grave person does carries weight. Whether a matter is great or small, its importance and weight depend on whose hands it is in. In the hands of a grave person, even a small matter will be taken seriously by others. Conversely, in the hands of a light person, a significant matter will be considered by others as inconsequential. In learning to be grave, first, one should not express his opinions lightly; second, one should not judge or criticize flippantly; and third, one should speak slowly and accurately. It is not that one should be silent but that one should speak with discretion.

He who is grave is protected, for evil temptations do not come to him easily. Especially in the case of a young woman, gravity brings protection, while lightness invites harm.

Be affectionate, ardent, and accommodating toward others, and conduct yourself with gravity.

CHAPTER TWO

UNDERSTANDING CHARACTER

THE IMPORTANCE OF CHARACTER

Whereas our words represent our person, our character is our very person. A person's usefulness, the things which can be entrusted to him, the responsibilities he can bear, and the things he is able to accomplish altogether depend on his character. A carpenter determines the use of a piece of wood based on its quality. Laziness ruins one's usefulness. Accordingly, character has very much to do with the Lord's service. Consider those persons in the Bible whom God used. They were used by God because they possessed a character that was fit for His use. Their character was simply their person. They became persons useful to God because their character could be used by Him. Since Abraham, Moses, and Paul all had an excellent character, God greatly used them. The destiny of our usefulness to the Lord hinges on our character. Whether we are useful before God depends upon the suitability of our human character.

THE CONSTITUTION OF CHARACTER

Our character is constituted of our inborn nature plus our acquired habits. Whereas disposition is inborn, character is cultivated. A person's character is thirty percent nature and seventy percent habit. For this reason, a young person must pay full attention to character building. A person over the age of fifty has a set personality with a definite pattern that has been developed over his lifetime. In a young person, more inborn nature than acquired habit is manifested. As he grows older, he displays less of his nature and more of his habits. Consequently, acquired habits are more important than inborn nature. Generally, the character of a person over the

age of twenty already contains more habit than nature. Never
neglect your daily living, for it builds up your habits. For
example, if a child is placed in a Chinese home, he will be cast
into a Chinese mold. The same child placed in a family of
another nationality will resemble a person of that nationality
when he grows up. In considering the matter of character, we
must give heed to our daily life, which is able to mold our
character. The suitability of our character to God determines
our usefulness to God.

THE CHARACTER ESSENTIAL
FOR THE LORD'S SERVICE

1. Genuine—Being the Same Within and Without

What is genuineness? It denotes a consistency within and
without. In many instances no lying is involved, but there
certainly is an absence of genuineness. A person who is not
genuine is useless in the Lord's hand. Moses was a most genuine person. When he came down from Mount Sinai, he broke
the two tablets in anger. He was the same within and without.
It is impossible to find a case in the Bible where Moses was
not consistent through and through. A genuine person is solid
and trustworthy. This does not mean, however, that a person
should be free to lose his temper. To behave in a pleasant way
when you are actually irate is to pretend and to be false.
Some people speak on a subject to two people in two different
ways. While they may not have the intention to deceive, they
do not speak genuinely. Those who serve the Lord must cultivate a genuine character. In confronting certain matters, we
may refrain from speaking anything because of our fear of
God. However, if we do speak, we must be genuine.

2. Exact—Being Absolutely Accurate

It is very difficult to be exact with respect to time, words,
and numbers. Many things are done in a "just-to-get-by"
manner. This "more-or-less" attitude is most damaging. A
person must not be "more-or-less"; he must be accurate.
Accomplishing ninety-nine percent of a task, leaving one
percent undone, is the same as not having done it at all. We

should develop a character that is not sloppy but absolutely accurate. We must be exact both in word and in deed.

3. Strict—Taking Matters Seriously

Genuineness makes one solid, and exactness makes one strong. Strictness is the practice of genuineness and exactness. Genuineness and exactness can never be practiced by a loose person. To do everything genuinely and exactly requires a strict character. Whatever passes through the hands of a loose person becomes somewhat inaccurate and lacking in genuineness. Because a loose person is not strict, whatever he says must be discounted. Even his study of the Bible is sloppy. Those who are strict receive light while studying the Bible. They never let things go. When problems arise, they proceed to solve them, always tracing to the root of the matter. A loose person, who usually is curious and lives in his imagination, can never solve problems. A strict person never meddles in matters that do not concern him, nor does he entertain idle thoughts. He performs his task seriously and accurately.

4. Diligent—Not Slothful

A strict person is always diligent. Diligence is the most important characteristic of a servant of the Lord. The Bible is full of teachings concerning diligence. In Romans chapter twelve, Paul mentions consecration, serving in coordination, and gifts, and follows his word with "not slothful in zeal" (v. 11). One must be diligent in service. Diligence is crucial because it builds up our spiritual reserve and thus enriches us. Spiritual wealth comes from diligence. Laziness invariably produces poverty. He who is diligent is always soberminded, whereas he who is lazy is usually muddleheaded. All things exist in time. A successful person is one who seizes his time. We must redeem our lost time. Laziness is detestable because it causes our being to be squandered. It swallows our time and will eventually devour our whole life.

Diligence, however, cannot be a matter of legality or of regulation; it should be practiced spontaneously. We should be the same whether seen or unseen by others. As a person becomes diligent, he will require much more of himself. One who is lazy can never clean thoroughly, because he is stiff-backed and will not even bend his waist to sweep the floor. An unconcerned person is lazy, but he who is concerned yet does not take action is a person who has not been dealt with. Only the diligent know to work. The Lord's servant must cultivate a diligent character and never let himself go easily. Then he will be able to handle whatever God entrusts to him. Only those who are diligent can do the Lord's work. The more a person works, the more he will become humble, practical, and careful, and the more he will control his temper and reject his flesh. This is most profitable before God. One who is diligent finishes thoroughly all the work that is around him and has been committed to him.

D. L. Moody said, "I have yet to see a lazy person get saved." Some people are actually too lazy to believe and to ask; thus, they miss such a great matter as their salvation. It is difficult to find a slothful person who has much spiritual pursuit.

5. Broad—Having a Wide Perspective

A person who practices being genuine, exact, strict, and diligent can very easily become narrow. By nature all sloppy people are broad. However, those who serve the Lord need to be broad in their character. The heart of Solomon was as broad as the sand on the seashore. Since the sand surrounds the sea, it must be broader than the sea. We must practice being broad. Only people who are broad can discover the great things in the Bible. A narrow person can only study the trivial matters and give messages on minor topics; further-more, he may even make a message on a major topic become insignificant. A worker must learn to be broad, to study the Bible with a broad perspective, and to study the great items in the Scriptures. He must learn to pay attention to the sig-nificant things and to be magnanimous toward people. Such a person commands a wide view, and his leading of others and his knowledge of the Lord are likewise broad.

6. Fine—Not Careless or Negligent

Although we should not be narrow, we should be fine. In the last two thousand years, those who were greatly used by the Lord were both broad and fine. Those who were narrow and coarse were invariably of little use. The Lord leads us according to the grace that God gives us. Too often, however, His leading is dependent on our character. Some brothers and sisters can study the Bible and pray, but they cannot bear responsibilities. Because of their character, we dare not entrust the Lord's business to them. They receive much grace and know how to pray, but they have not built up the proper character that enables them to accomplish things. Although they may be placed in some areas of service, they cannot be entrusted with the service. The service of the Lord requires a broad and fine person. To study the Bible well, one must find the scriptural basis of any matter with a broad and fine eye.

7. Stable—Steady, Not Easily Moved or Changed, and Not Panicky

To be stable is to be steady, immovable, and unchangeable. What a stable life the Lord lived on the earth! He was not stirred by His brothers' suggestion that He go up to Jerusalem to gain recognition, and when His opposers tried to stone Him, He walked past them straightly. Had we been in that situation, we either would have been stoned or would have quickly fled. Once the Lord knew that Lazarus was sick, He remained in the same place for two days more. Our Lord never wavered. He was stable. Those who know God's will do not panic. An unstable person is like a reed in the wilderness blown by the wind. Never steady or stable, he leans west when blown by the east wind and east when blown by the west wind. A person who fluctuates can never understand the will of God. He can neither work with others nor serve the church.

However, to be stable is not to be slow. Stability includes not speaking uncertainly or doing things about which one is unsure. A stable person is not easily changed by his environment. He controls his time well and takes action only after he has waited and is sure of God's will. To be stable is not to be stubborn, stiff-necked, or obstinate, but to have an inner quality that is immovable and unchangeable. Luther was a stable and strong person; therefore, God could use him. Stability is an important qualification in serving the Lord and in selecting

a co-worker. Time works, but only with a stable person. Once
a stable person realizes God's will, he will act immediately,
regardless of the cost. Yet until God's time has come, no one is
able to influence him. Hence, we need to learn to be stable.
Panicking does not help. We must remain steady through the
storm, knowing that when it is over, the difficulties also will
cease. Those riding in a boat well understand the importance
of stability. When riding in a small boat on a stormy sea, one
simply cannot afford to panic.

8. Deep—Searching Downward and Digging Deeper, Not Being Superficial

The book of Proverbs says that a foolish person is a shallow person. The observation of a shallow person is not
accurate. His understanding of the church, people, matters,
and things is superficial. Being deep is closely related to
being thorough and serious. A shallow person always makes
superficial observations, whereas a deep person always
searches and digs when he looks at things. To a shallow
person, it may seem that there is nothing to do, even if a
church is committed to him. While others have much to speak
in a message, he has nothing to say. While others labor to
obtain light in studying the Bible, he is satisfied with merely
a literal understanding. In listening to people, a deep person
does not easily believe others and listens beyond superficial
remarks. However, a shallow person readily believes others'
words, and his relaying of information is often inconsistent
and incomplete. As a result, gossip is created. Those who
serve the Lord must be deep in truth, in experience, and in
leading others. A shallow person cannot serve the Lord,
because he will make God's work shallow. Those who like to
represent others are shallow people. One who is deep is
neither complicated nor shallow. Such a person is three-
dimensional, always investigating and researching.

9. Patient—Being Able to Wait and Not Being Anxious

According to James chapter five, the farmer who wishes to
obtain the fruit of the earth cannot be anxious (v. 7); he must

wait for the appointed time. A patient person can wait. Contrary to the common understanding, patience is different from endurance. To be patient is not to be slothful and sloppy but to work diligently without anxiety. Everything we do takes time. The amount of effort put forth will determine how much one can accomplish. No work can be done cheaply. Those who hope for instant accomplishments can never do the work of God. To do God's work a person must work daily yet without anxiety. A patient person is not distracted by anything temporary, since he knows his commission. This is like the farmer, to whom waiting is normal: on one hand, he works in the fields; on the other hand, he waits. In leading others one may often be disappointed, but those who are patient never give up hope. When our work suffers a setback, we must be patient. Time will prove and time will tell. Time will vindicate and manifest the truth. The manifestation of the glory of God may be only half a minute away.

One should be aggressive but not anxious. This requires practice. A character produced out of patience is invaluable. We should not draw conclusions quickly concerning people or matters. After only a few more days of waiting, the real situation will emerge. We must learn to be patient when we are in need. If we are patient when in need, we will never have to borrow. When Paul wrote to the Corinthians, though he felt heavy and pressed, he was nonetheless patient. Those who serve the Lord must possess such a quality. Many people make a clamor over minor hardships, make known their smallest problem, and make an instant judgment concerning any matter which comes their way. Such are useless people. To be patient is to wait. It is different from being slow. Whether one has a quick or a slow disposition, one must learn to be patient. To be slow is to fail to grasp opportunities; this must be dealt with. A patient person is prompt and nimble. We should be patient before opportunity arises and should grasp it immediately when it does. As we serve the church daily, we should wait patiently concerning all the situations which confront us and concerning the results of our work. Before the harvest season arrives, we should not be anxious; neither should we relax and be lazy. We should be full of feelings toward people and things. We should be sensitive and concerned and should have proper foresight. We must finish whatever work we have to do and leave the rest to time. In many ways time represents God.

Those who would be proper persons, and especially be weighty in the hand of the Lord, must possess all of the preceding nine characteristics. Without these nine qualities, we will not be enlightened in our study of the Bible; neither will we meet the requirements of the spiritual life in our dealings with people, things, and the Lord's work. Also, it is very unlikely that we will have much spiritual growth. Our being must correspond with the work we wish to accomplish, and our character must match the business we plan to do. In a character that is fit for the Lord's use, acquired habits are much more important than inborn nature. This all depends on the building up of a character that is suitable to the Lord.

CHAPTER THREE

EXAMPLES OF A PROPER CHARACTER

Scripture Reading: Mark 1:35; 3:20-21; 6:30-31, 34; 8:1-10

In this chapter we shall consider what kind of character the Lord Jesus had while He was on the earth. We may think that those of us who serve the Lord need to have a proper character, but that the Lord Jesus had no such need. However, if we read the four Gospels carefully, we can see that while the Lord was on the earth, His service before God depended greatly on His character.

THE EXAMPLE OF THE LORD'S CHARACTER

Among the four Gospels, the Gospel of Mark especially shows us how the Lord Jesus served God. All those who study the Bible can perceive in this Gospel the character of the Servant of God. In reading the Gospel of John, we can realize the life that was in Jesus Christ—the life of the Son of God. By studying the Gospel of Luke, we can see the perfect disposition within that perfect Man. If we study the Gospel of Matthew, we can witness how the King of the kingdom of the heavens conducted Himself. When we read the Gospel of Mark, we can notice the character of the Servant of God. In the Gospel of John the Lord shows us by His living on the earth the life that was within Him. In the Gospel of Luke, the Lord reveals to us His human disposition by living as a man on the earth. As a man His disposition was perfect and beautiful. In the Gospel of Mark, however, the Lord is seen as a servant. There He did not display His life or His disposition but His character.

In seeking for a friend, you would often look for a pleasing disposition, not necessarily a proper character, in the other party. Usually, your only concern is his disposition and not his character. For example, a person does not have to be an early riser to qualify to be your friend. He may regularly get up and go to bed on time, but if his disposition is not pleasant, you will not want to make friends with him. Therefore, in making friends you first pay attention to a person's disposition. However, when you hire someone to do housework, do you care only for his personality? Certainly not. He may be very gentle, patient, loving, and moderate, but if he is also very lazy, sloppy, slow, and forgetful, would you hire him? When we consider employing someone, we should consider not only his disposition but also his character. Gentleness and kindness are in his disposition. But he still must be diligent, girded in his work, and always in his place, all of which are needed in his character.

If you are able to distinguish between disposition and character, you will find the matter of disposition in the Gospel of Luke and the matter of character in the Gospel of Mark. The Gospel of Luke reveals the disposition of a perfect Man. The Gospel of Mark unveils the character of the Servant of God. I say this with good reason. For example, Mark indicates on at least two occasions that the Lord Jesus did not even have time to eat. This is not recorded in Luke, John, or Matthew. Matthew speaks of the Lord as the King of the kingdom of the heavens; whether the King ate or not is unimportant. This matter was recorded only by Mark. In the Gospel of Mark there are these words: "And rising very early in the morning, while it was still night, He went out and went away to a desolate place, and there He prayed." The Lord was so busy serving others that He did not care to eat, giving people the impression that He was crazy. When He saw the crowd, He did not have the heart to send them away, fearing that they would faint on the way. So He gave them bread and fish to satisfy them. He even asked the disciples to gather the leftovers. Then, after He sent the people away, He left. Is it not significant that the Holy Spirit recorded these things? The book of Mark shows us that God had found a Person on the earth whose character was fit for God's service. In other words, this book demonstrates to us the character of the Lord Jesus as the Servant of God. Because He had such a character, He was useful in the hand of God in His service to God and to man.

One can observe the character of the Lord Jesus as God's Servant in every chapter and every paragraph of the book of Mark. Although on a certain day He healed many sick ones, cast out many demons, did much work, and went to sleep late, He still rose very early the next morning to pray. Such was His diligence. When He was busy, He cared only for others' needs and not for His own hunger. This is the character which one who serves the Lord should possess. When the multitudes gathered in the wilderness and it was late, He could not bear to send them away for fear that they would be exhausted from lack of food. Whereas this incident was recorded in a brief way in the other Gospels, it was recounted in the Gospel of Mark in great detail. That record shows us that He not only cared for the crowd, but He also thoroughly discerned and understood the whole situation. Further, He knew how to arrange things. He calmly charged the people to sit down row by row, took the bread and the fish, blessed them, and distributed them row by row. After the people were filled, the disciples gathered the fragments in baskets. Then He sent the people away and brought the disciples to another place. Does this record describe a miracle of the Lord? Does it unveil the life of the Lord? Does it reveal the disposition of the Lord? No. This shows us His character. He was diligent, considerate, perceptive, sympathetic, and concerned for others, and He never shirked responsibility. Without the character in the Gospel of Mark, the life in the Gospel of John could not be dispensed. In order to be dispensed, the life recorded in the book of John needed the character in the book of Mark. The life in John is the food; the character in Mark is the container.

We lack this kind of character today. I have observed that some of the brothers are often wasteful in their service. To be wasteful is a small matter. But I am afraid that when these brothers serve the Lord, souls will be lost. This is a serious problem. Do you think the Lord treasured the twelve baskets of fragments? No, the Lord wanted to show the disciples that one who works for God in service to Him must do things in this manner. The Lord trained the disciples and led them that they also might have this kind of character. We must see that in the matter of serving the Lord and being a servant of God, the one thing that is indispensable is a proper character. We cannot serve God without a good character.

EXAMPLES OF THE APOSTLES' CHARACTER

In the Apostle Paul's writings in his Epistles concerning the Lord Jesus, we can actually see the writer himself. Though all of Paul's Epistles concern Christ, they allow us to see Paul. I do not think that the Epistles of Peter need to be designated as such. By reading them one can immediately recognize their writer. The same is true of Paul's writings. We can see the apostles from the epistles they wrote, because it was Christ whom they bore, and it was Christ who lived through them. Moses saw the vision of fire burning on the thorn-bush. All the Epistles by the apostles were written according to this principle. On the one hand, Christ used Paul as His upholder, putting Himself on Paul. On the other hand, Paul lived out Christ. Because of these two points, each time they spoke concerning Christ, the apostles could not avoid being seen.

There are two lines in the Bible. One line concerns the upholding of Christ, and the other, the living out of Christ. To live out Christ is a matter of life, whereas to uphold Christ is a matter of character. With every apostle there are the matters of character and life. With regard to Paul's character, he was used by Christ; he bore Christ, and Christ was upheld by him. As to life, Paul took Christ as his life; he lived in Christ, and Christ lived in him. Thus, when we read the Epistles of Paul, it is not difficult to see that some matters in them are related to character and some to life. For example, Paul said, "What do you want? Shall I come to you with a rod, or in love and a spirit of meekness?" (1 Cor. 4:21); he also said, "Who is weak, and I am not weak? Who is stumbled, and I do not burn?" (2 Cor. 11:29), and, "But when Cephas came to Antioch I opposed him to his face, because he was to be condemned" (Gal. 2:11). These words reflect a certain character. On the other hand, Paul said, "Always bearing about in the body the putting to death of Jesus, that the life also of Jesus might be manifested in our body" (2 Cor. 4:10), and also, "And we all with unveiled face, beholding and reflecting as a mirror the glory of the Lord, are being transformed into the same image from glory to glory, even as from the Lord Spirit" (2 Cor. 3:18). These words refer to life. In certain parts of the Epistles of Paul we find his character as a servant of God: strong, responsible, serious, intolerant of errors, honest, willing to rebuke others to their face. In other places we see the very life which he lived. We should not have only life without a proper character; neither can we have only a good character without life.

One day in Manila, during a car ride with some brothers to the countryside, we saw an elegant Catholic cathedral situated on a small hill. The brothers brought me into the place for a visit. When I entered, I saw several nuns dressed in white, kneeling. They were motionless and appeared unreal until I looked carefully. They were so adept in the practice that they did not move even a little. We watched them for a long time before one stood up. We were transfixed as we observed the way she walked. Such serenity and composure would be impossible to imitate. As she went forward to get a Bible, her stride, posture, and movements commanded our utmost respect and admiration. What marvelous conduct! If I had not known the Lord, I would have resolved that day to join Catholicism. I believe that if some unbelievers were to see those nuns and us, they would surely conclude that we Christians are not as respectable as the Catholics. However, those who know Christ would realize that such conduct was not life; it was a developed character at best. A good character devoid of life is of no value. But life without a proper character is equally useless. Regardless of how much we know about Christ, we cannot minister Christ without a proper character.

THE NECESSITY OF CHARACTER BUILDING FOR THE LORD'S SERVICE

What kind of work are we planning to do? Do we expect to do a work that is valuable and weighty or a work that is shallow? In the Lord's service there is the need not only of the knowledge of the Lord but also of a character that upholds the Lord. The Bible requires that the elders be grave. Is this a matter of character or of life? It is too clear that this is a matter of character and not of life. One person may be clearly saved but still frivolous. Another may oppose the Lord Jesus yet be serious in his character. If these two people were to stand up and speak to a crowd, which one would gain the confidence of the people? It would be the opposer. Why? Because he is sober. We can immediately realize from this illustration that our usefulness in the Lord's hand is based on our character and that it takes our character to minister life. Obviously, without life nothing is ministered, but without a proper character, life still cannot be dispensed.

Admittedly, we are short in life, but I feel strongly that there is a severe, even desperate, lack in our character. For example, according to my observation, some young brothers are totally unlearned in manners. In their contact with people they seem to have no sense of who is older and who is younger. They consider showing respect as shameful and politeness as undemocratic. They care little whether the person in their presence is a school principal or a dean. Be assured that such people are finished; they cannot serve the Lord.

Young brothers, in the dormitory where you live, are you polite toward your schoolmates? Although I did not visit you every day, based on my limited observations, I know how you live. Please forgive me for saying that you do not have the proper character at all. I admit that you may not fight or quarrel; I also dare say that your character has not been built up. To build up your character, you must keep the rules governing which bed you should sleep in, where you should hang your clothes, and where you should store your suitcase. You must abide by the rules of the school. You may think that these are small matters, but if you are not exercised in these things in your daily life, you will be absolutely useless to God. You will lack the character of rule-keeping. You may freely throw your shoes under another's bed and hang your shirt on his bedpost, and his vest may somehow turn up in your area. Believe me, this kind of person can never do a work.

Rule-keeping is on the passive side. Positively, we need to be polite. We should rush to do the unpleasant jobs and let others do the easy ones. This is not life; it is merely the sign of a good character. But if such a character is not built up in us, we cannot hope to serve the Lord properly. If you are not a regulated person, your preaching will likewise be undisciplined. If you are disorderly, what you preach will also be disorganized.

Brothers, in serving the Lord character is no less important than life. Without a proper character, you have no way to do a work. Life is your material and character is your technique. A carpenter cannot make anything without wood; but this does not mean that he can make something as long as there is wood. The saw may be useful in the hand of another but not in yours. The ax is useful to others, but in your hand it only ruins the wood. You do not have a particular character simply because you have never practiced. As a rule, if you are about to go through a door and a younger brother wants to do the same, you should let him go first. If you are carrying a basin and some water happens to spill on your roommate's bed, you must wipe the waterdrops quickly and look for an opportunity to apologize to him. I do not recognize this as life, yet if you desire to serve the Lord, you must be particular about your character. The character within you enables you to be disciplined in your service to the Lord.

THE DIFFERENCE AND RELATIONSHIP
BETWEEN CHARACTER AND LIFE

Let me further illustrate the difference between character and life. Consider a sister who loves to gossip, talks a great deal, and is always unhappy with others. Such a condition indicates a shortage in life, not in character. Another sister rarely speaks or becomes angry, because both her tongue and her flesh have received the dealing of the cross. However, she is sloppy in her living and inconveniences those around her. When others murmur, she is not angry and does not blame them. This sister may be excellent in life, but she lacks one thing—a proper character. This example shows the difference between the aspect of life and the aspect of character.

Nevertheless, we must realize that life and character are not independent of each other. Life can influence our character, and on many occasions it can even replace our character. But character cannot affect life or substitute for life. Often the spirituality of a spiritual person becomes his character and replaces his character. This was the case with the Lord Jesus. The character of the Lord Jesus was almost an expression of His life. We may say that the aspects of the Lord's character, as recorded in Mark, were the expression of His life. In other words, much of His life was also His character.

However, we cannot say that character is life, for even an unbeliever has his character. For example, the sobriety of a certain person is part of his character, not his life. The spirituality of a spiritual person, which issues from his abiding in the Lord, can make him sober. The character of a Christian should not merely be character. We should not only display outward sobriety, thoroughness, and consideration for others, with no life inwardly. We must have both life and character. In fact, we should go one step further: our life and our character should be blended as one. Although character does not equal life, life can become a great part of our character. I am polite because I live in Christ; I am also sober because I live in Christ. I can be careful because Christ is my carefulness, and I can be regulated because Christ is my regulation. Life and character have become one in me.

In the beginning the person who loves the Lord often seeks after life. Gradually he realizes that it is his character which limits his dispensing of the Lord to others. Then he changes the way he conducts himself; that is, he begins to develop his character. At first this kind of character building is mostly man-made. As he grows in the Lord and the life in him becomes strengthened, his character is slowly brought into life. Eventually, the life within him is mingled with his outward character. At this point his outward sobriety comes from his inward life. His outward politeness and orderliness are also issues of the life within him. His character is constituted predominantly with the inward element of life. This was true of our Lord when He was on the earth, and it must have been true of Paul. Today, our need before the Lord is to pay attention to the fact that in serving the Lord, without life we have nothing to minister to others. Likewise, if we only have life but lack the proper character, we have no way to minister. In the Lord's service there is the need for life as well as the proper character. Therefore, we must thoroughly build up our character and our human conduct.

CHAPTER FOUR

CHARACTER BUILDING

Scripture Reading: 2 Cor. 3:5-6; 4:2-3

In this chapter we will cover the things that a serving one should build up before the Lord. To be useful in the Lord's hand, one who serves Him must first be properly built up.

THE TWO ASPECTS OF BEING USED BY THE LORD

We have said that if a person desires to be used by the Lord, he must realize that his natural life is unuseable in the Lord's hand and that he himself is totally corrupt before the Lord. The natural life is nothing but a thorn-bush, and the self is nothing but leprosy. However, every truth in the Bible is twofold, showing us something in one aspect and then something else in another aspect. Both aspects are true. Any doctrine that is not two-sided is defective. Concerning our being useful in the Lord's hand, there are two aspects. One aspect about which we have heard much is the tearing down of the self. Formerly you may have felt that you were talented and very capable or that you were better than others. But now you have seen a vision that your natural life is nothing but a thorn-bush and your self, nothing but leprosy. Once you realize this, you will spontaneously fall down and collapse. To collapse is to be broken. Actually, God always shines upon us and leads us in the principle of breaking. On one hand, the Bible shows us that a person who serves God must be adequately broken. It is true that his natural life, self, temperament, and disposition need to be touched by the Lord, broken, and torn down. On the other hand, the Bible shows us that something must be built up in a person who serves the Lord. This building up refers not only to the inward consti-tution of the Lord's life but also to the development of his character. What does this mean? We must cover this in more detail.

First, we need to see that God would never use what is of us for the work that He wants us to do, just as the flame of fire burned upon the thorn-bush without consuming it. We cannot add anything to God's work. However, when God does use us, we must be fit for His use. Although the thorn-bush was not the material which fueled the fire, it nevertheless upheld and showed forth the flames. Brothers and sisters, please remember that when God uses you to accomplish His work, you cannot add anything of your own, since all that you have does not avail in God's work. Yet on the other hand, it may be questionable whether you can be used by the Lord and whether His work can be carried out through you.

For example, when I put a Bible, a hymnal, and a cup of water on a table, the table will never add a drop of water to my cup, a verse or a chapter to my Bible, or a hymn to my hymnal. But here is a problem: if the table is tilted, I will not be able to put a cup on it. In one sense I do not use the table at all, because it does not add anything to my Bible, my cup, or my hymnal. However, there is the question of whether I am able to place my Bible, cup, or hymnal steadily on the table.

So never assume that you are clear about the Lord's teaching and say, "Well, we are just thorn-bushes; we have no function in God's work, and we cannot add glow to His fire. We are just persons upon whom God's flame can burn as brightly as He desires. Anyway, He does not use us as fuel. We are merely bushes with no responsibility." I am afraid that many saints hold such a concept. If you do, you are wrong. It is true that the table does not add anything to the contents of the Bible, hymnal, or cup when I put them on top of it. However, if the table is not set properly, so that it is level and stable, I will not be able to use it at all. On one hand, I do not utilize anything of the table, yet on the other hand, I must use it. Similarly, even though God does not use what is of us, our proper condition and situation qualify us to be used by Him.

Remember, whether the flames of God will burn upon a particular thorn-bush is a conditional matter. Do not assume that God will burn upon any thorn-bush. This is not so. God's fire can burn upon Moses but not necessarily upon you. Although God did not use Moses as the fuel, He could burn upon him. However, He may not be able to burn upon you.

We should acknowledge that we can contribute absolutely nothing to what God wants to produce in us. Paul said, "Not that we are sufficient of ourselves to account anything as of ourselves, but our sufficiency is of God, who also made us sufficient as ministers of a new covenant, not of letter, but of the Spirit" (2 Cor. 3:5-6). This means that whatever Paul had could never be added into God's holy fire. He also said, "We have this treasure in earthen vessels, that the excellence of the power may be of God and not of us" (2 Cor. 4:7). This power comes entirely from the treasure, and not at all from us. On the other hand, Paul also said, "Therefore, having this ministry, as we received mercy...we have renounced the hidden things of shame, not walking in craftiness nor adulterating the word of God, but by the manifestation of the truth commending ourselves to every man's conscience before God" (2 Cor. 4:1-2). While Paul confessed to his own insufficiency, he also told us that he bore much responsibility. We can readily see here that God used Paul, though not the things of Paul.

Having seen the principle, we shall now consider a few practical matters. For example, if we are doing the Lord's work among the Chinese-speaking people in Taiwan, can we be illiterate in Chinese? Surely we cannot. "Why not?" you may ask. "If the fire which burned upon the bush had no need of the bush as its fuel, why do I need to know Chinese? Literate or not, I am still a bush. What difference does literacy make?"

This illustrates that although the fire burning upon the bush does not use the bush as its fuel, there still is the need to pay attention to the bush itself. For God to give His complete and detailed set of laws to the Israelites, He needed a servant like Moses. Every student of law considers the Roman law a requirement in his studies, and the Roman law derived its principles from the Old Testament. Even until now, no law is more complete or more lofty than the law of Moses, because the law written by Moses was from God. The question is this:

had Moses not been educated with the knowledge of that time but rather had been an unlearned peasant, do you think God could have used him? I absolutely believe not.

When I was first saved, I met some people who had the idea that education was unnecessary. They thought that if we have God's love, all is well; it is completely useless to be educated. This is a wrong concept. Undoubtedly, it is the fire that burns upon the bush, but still the bush must be qualified in order for God to ignite this fire upon it. Some thorn-bushes meet the requirements, whereas others do not. The flame of God's deliverance of the Israelites and the giving of the law could burn only upon Moses, and on no one else, because there was no other person who was qualified.

In this chapter we are considering the need for character building in order that some could meet the requirements. God does not need you as the fuel, but when He uses you, you must have the proper qualifications. To be useable, a table must be level and stable. A carpenter must work on it, attach four legs, and polish the surface. This is the building work of a carpenter to make it a suitable piece of furniture.

According to our continuous observation, we must conclude that many brothers and sisters are of little use to God because they are ill-qualified for His use. They are like a table that is not quite straight, upright, level, or stable. God's fire could burn upon Moses but not upon them, because Moses was qualified for God's burning, whereas they are not.

I would like to give another example. Suppose there is a downpour today and you have put several basins under the building's eaves to collect rainwater. All the basins will be filled within a short time. However, if some of the basins are cracked and full of holes, could any water stay in them? No. The leaking simply offsets the filling, and regardless of how much it rains, all the water that comes into the basins will eventually run out. It is easy to see that these containers are inadequate. Suppose some other basins are not merely broken and leaking but are almost flat. Surely all the water will run off despite the continuous rain. Such basins do not meet the requirements for holding water. We need water to bathe, wash clothes, and water the plants. It is true that the basins themselves cannot produce water, and it is true that what we actually use is the water and not the basins. We use the water all year long. We do not use anything from the basins except the water that falls into them. Nevertheless, from another viewpoint, the ability of the basins to hold water depends on whether they meet the requirements. Some are able to hold water, whereas others are not.

Brothers and sisters, are you a basin with holes, a broken basin, or a flat one? There must be a certain building up in a person who serves God. The dimension of depth must be added to the flat surface, and all the leaks and cracks must be patched. Furthermore, your capacity must be enlarged. As a basin, you may be able to hold four gallons of water on the first day. After four days you may hold eight gallons, and then twenty gallons in another ten days. Originally, you may be only three inches tall. Two days later you may extend to one foot. Brothers and sisters, remember that the extent of our usefulness to God depends on the extent of His building work in us. The amount of building up in us determines the measure of our usefulness to Him. If God does not find us built up, He cannot use us.

Now let us discuss a few matters that need to be built up in us. They are all essential. We will not be useful to God if we lack even one of them.

THE MATTER OF EDUCATION

At the very least, one who wishes to be used by God must certainly receive some education. It is difficult for an unlearned person who has not developed his mind through education to be useful to God. Being educated is a condition that we must fulfill in order for God to use us. Although we all seem to acknowledge this fact, I still need to add a few words.

We have not paid adequate attention to language learning. In principle, we all should have considered this when we were young. For instance, there are some who cannot read reference materials in foreign languages. This is a big problem. Students of the sciences used to be required to read German because most of the scientific publications were in that language. It was not that they liked to speak German; rather, they needed to research the scientific materials in German. Similarly, throughout church history spiritual materials were written either in Hebrew, Greek, Latin, or English. To use these reference materials, you must know these languages. For this reason, the young people should study Hebrew, Greek, and English. They need to study some of these languages in order to use the reference books.

Moreover, I have discovered from the writings of some brothers and sisters that even their Chinese is inadequate. Actually, our language need not be complex or elegant but simply understandable and expressive of our thoughts. This matter also affects our usefulness in God's hand.

Brothers and sisters, if you can use a reference book in Greek, read English, and write fluently in Chinese, you will see how much your usefulness will multiply in the Lord's hand. Regretfully, you have not paid attention to this and have wasted much time. As a rule you should spend one hour each day studying a language. In a year you will be able to use reference materials in Hebrew. Similar proficiency in Greek will require only half a year. If you spend an hour a day studying English, you will be able to do translation work in three years. Since it is more difficult to translate from Chinese to English, an ability to translate from English to Chinese will be sufficient. If we do not build ourselves up in such matters, we reduce our usefulness in God's work.

However, this is still not my point. My point is actually character development, a matter which I fear many have ignored.

THE MEANING OF CHARACTER

When we speak of a person's character, it is difficult to say whether it is a matter of the spirit, the soul, or the body. Actually, it involves all three. For instance, laziness is a problem of character. Some may say that it is a matter of habit; actually, it is a matter of character. Is it the spirit that is lazy, or is it the soul or the body? It is difficult to say. The spirit, the soul, and the body are all lazy. This is a problem of character. Consider another example: some people are so sloppy that they confuse the book of Mark with the book of Matthew and the book of Matthew with Galatians. If we ask them how many chapters there are in the Gospel of Matthew, they will answer that there are sixteen. While some people are this careless, others take things most seriously and perform their work meticulously. These are all matters of character.

I agree that a person who does not have a strong spirit is of little use in the Lord's hand. The same is true of one who lacks a strong mind and a clear understanding, and of one who is weak physically. We need to be built up in our spirit, soul, and body before we can be useful to God. However, what we are discussing here concerns neither the spirit, nor the soul, nor the body, but character. If your character is deficient, you will not be of much use in the Lord's hand. What then is character? It is the way you behave as a person, plus the person behind such behavior. A person's character is his disposition which has become his way of living.

We have mentioned that character is composed of two things: inborn nature and acquired habits. A newborn child has only an inborn nature, not acquired habits. But you and I have both. We may say that nature is the skeleton and habits are the flesh and the skin. Together, they form one's character. If we send a Chinese child to America as soon as he is born, when he grows up he will be full of American temperament. We can see from this that a person's acquired habits are more influential than his inborn nature. When our inborn nature combined with our acquired habits become the way we live, the result is our character. Our character affects our usefulness to God more than our spirit, soul, and body.

When I began to serve the Lord, I did not understand this matter, and it did not seem important. In helping the brothers and sisters, I would merely tell them to study the Bible diligently, pray much, and be dealt with before the Lord. I still admit that these points definitely have their usefulness and place. But I have seen persons who prayed, studied the Bible, and pursued the Lord fervently who were not of much use to God. In the past I noticed only the result but not the cause. Now I have discovered the nullifying factor: a faulty character prevents such persons from being useful. Their character has canceled the effectiveness of their Bible study and prayer.

Dear brothers and sisters, neither your spirit, nor your soul, nor your body can replace you; nearly your whole being exists in your character. Allow me to say that, because your character is deficient, merely to have a strong spirit is not adequate. I once knew a sister and was quite familiar with her situation. She loved the Lord very much, pursued after Him, and spent time in prayer, Bible reading, and meetings. Nevertheless, one could not find much usefulness in her. Previously I was perplexed by this. Gradually I found out that it was due to an undeveloped character. Although she could pray in her room for one to two hours, and pray in a good way, once she began to take care of business, meet people, and deal with things, she was altogether sloppy. When she conversed with others, what she spoke usually differed from what she thought. Then, when asked, she inevitably denied that she had spoken a certain thing. Did she intentionally lie, or did she purposely deceive? No, that was simply her way of behaving. Please consider, could God use a person with such a character? No, absolutely not. Now we see what character is and how character is related to our usefulness. Please remember that God does not use what is of you in His work, but He needs you as His means to work. If you are not thus qualified, God cannot use you.

Let me give you another small example, something which I have observed many times. I asked a brother to take a letter to another brother. After a few days I met him again and asked him whether he had delivered the message. He replied, "Oh, I completely forgot." Do not think that this is a small matter. It reveals his condition as well as his character. In principle, a person whose character has been dealt with and built up will first consider his own ability to do a job before he accepts a request. If he cannot do it, he will not accept the request; but if he is able, he will do it immediately. Either I should refuse a request, or I should accept it and carry it out, even if I must go to hell to do so. Do you think God can entrust anything to a person who will accept a request carelessly, but who will not fulfill his word afterwards? Can God entrust him with His work? In other words, can such a person receive God's commission or God's leading? Not at all.

LAZINESS

Many in the Lord's service have a big problem in their character—laziness. I have several points to cover concerning this matter. This is by no means a great doctrine, yet it has much to do with our usefulness to the Lord. The first characteristic of one who serves the Lord must be diligence. A lazy person is useless to God. Can you find a verse in the Bible which tells us that God spoke to Moses in the evening? On the contrary, in a number of instances God called Moses early and told him to go in the morning to a certain place to meet Pharaoh. Dear brothers and sisters, a slothful person can never be useful to God. Diligence must be built into our blood.

I do not wish to find fault with you, but I feel that I have a responsibility before the Lord to say this to you: some of you impress me as being lazy. There are many proofs of this. Forgive me for telling you that you are lazy. O brothers! O sisters! Allow me the liberty to say this, and believe what I say. I was once your age. I have also passed through what you are now learning and pursuing regarding the Lord's service. I am clear by watching you from the sidelines. I realize that you are not intentionally lazy but are so because there is not the element of diligence in your character. Because your past living, circumstances, and habits did not help to build diligence into your character, you now are short of it.

At this point I must ask all of you, even the Chinese people, to forgive me. Today, our country is not strong enough, not what it should be. We are making progress too slowly in politics, the economy, social condition, and education. Why is this? Rather than criticizing the leaders of the government, we must put the blame on our national character. We need to realize that the Chinese have a poor character. We are irresponsible, frivolous, and lazy; we pass the buck. With this kind of character, how can we succeed in building up a nation? I believe that our country would be strong if all those of average education were diligent.

My point is that since we Chinese are born in such a situation, when we serve God, we encounter many problems. As we have been raised in such an environment, if we are not completely revolutionized within, and if we bring our national character into the Lord's service, our service will never be successful. Such is an improper character. How deeply I am grieved concerning this matter. In our present condition, we would probably make a great work small and a small work disappear. This has everything to do with our character.

NOT BEING EARNEST

Another common condition is that most of you do not do things earnestly; you lack aggressiveness and simply try to get by. You always begin something without finishing it. Your belongings are disorderly. And when you say that you are short of time, it is because you are loose and waste time. If this is how you brothers and sisters do things, could your Bible study be any different? If you do things sloppily, how can you be careful in your Bible study? Your character will be the same in everything you do.

I have often criticized the way you dress. I do not refer to the quality of your clothing. I realize from the way you dress that there is a shortage in your character. Your carelessness and sloppiness are seen in the way you dress. If you are careless in dressing, could you be fine in Bible study? Could you do your work well? Could your work be prevailing, and could it produce valuable results? I do not believe so. What you do always reflects your character. I say again, unless this character is replaced and a new one built up, you will be useless in God's hand. O brothers, you must exercise yourself in these daily matters to build up something in yourself so that the divine fire can burn upon you.

Do not think that I am stressing outward things. Also, do not assume that to emphasize character is unspiritual. Are you genuinely spiritual with such a faulty character? Brothers and sisters, I say again, you must build up a proper character. Unless this is built up in you, your usefulness to the Lord will be limited.

I hope that from now on especially the young people will begin to build up a character that is useful to the Lord, so that every aspect of their living will be fit for the Lord's use.

The Lord Jesus said that one who is faithful in the least will be faithful in much (Luke 16:10). If your dress, your home, and the things you do reveal that you are a careless and passive person, how can your service to the Lord be aggressive? It is hardly possible. If you have not built up a proper character, you can give only an ordinary message, not a prevailing one. Your prayers also will be ordinary, not prevailing. They will be the same today as they were two years ago, showing no progress at all. Brothers, we must improve our character; otherwise, we will accomplish nothing. Even if we receive grace, we will not be able to minister that grace in spirit, because we are simply not qualified.

I realize that my speaking has been somewhat fragmented, but I hope that from now on you will seize every occasion, large and small, to build up your character so that you will be suitable for God's use. Because of your character, you do not receive any great light in reading the Bible, as others do. You would merely gloss over chapter one of the Gospel of Matthew, which speaks of Christ's genealogy. Why did Matthew speak of Christ's genealogy, whereas John did not? A person with a seeking character will definitely ask questions when he comes to this passage. May the Lord have mercy on us. I cannot speak too much in detail; I can only lay down a principle here. Just remember, our usefulness to God will be manifested only when we have a character suitable for His use.

CHAPTER FIVE

A CHARACTER USEFUL TO THE LORD

Scripture Reading: 2 Tim. 2:20, 21

In this chapter we will again consider the character of one who serves the Lord. In 2 Timothy 2:20-21 the apostle indicated that to be a servant of the Lord one must be "useful to the master." Literally, this means making one's service to the Lord both bountiful and practical. It is not a matter merely of being used or not used, but of how practical and how ample is the service. In other words, we should be those who serve practically and bountifully. This is what it means to be useful to the Master.

THE LORD NOT USING THE THINGS OF MAN

I would like to repeat: the Lord never uses what we have. This is the significance of the fire burning upon the bush without consuming the bush. The fire burned upon the bush but did not use the elements of the bush as fuel. Do not assume that your cleverness, wisdom, talent, and virtues can be the material for God to use. There is no such thing. Nothing of ours can contribute to our usefulness to the Lord. The Lord wants us to serve Him but not to minister what we have. Rather, He wants us to minister what He has. Ministering to others what we have in ourselves is most offensive to the Lord. As Paul indicated in 2 Corinthians 4, this is to preach ourselves, to minister ourselves, not the Lord, and it is condemned by Him.

In 2 Corinthians 3 Paul said that we are made sufficient as ministers of a new covenant, not of ourselves but of God. Then in chapter four he showed us not only that he was not made sufficient of himself but also that he did not preach himself; he preached Christ Jesus as Lord. Paul did not preach himself to others, nor did he minister himself to others. Paul preached and ministered Christ.

It was the same with Moses. Moses did not rely on his own ways to deal with Pharaoh; rather, it was God's authority manifested through Moses that dealt with Pharaoh. Pharaoh did not confront Moses' ability, talent, or wisdom, but he encountered in Moses something other than Moses, that is, the fire burning upon the bush.

The same principle applies to all those who served the Lord in both the Old and New Testaments. None of the prophets in the Old Testament, whether Jeremiah, Isaiah, Daniel, or any other, could bring his own cleverness, wisdom, or ability into the Lord's work. In other words, what those prophets preached was not their own ability, wisdom, or cleverness, but Jehovah, who came upon them, and the words of Jehovah. It is more so in the New Testament. Peter, James, John, and Paul could not add anything of themselves to the Lord's service. What they ministered to the saints and the churches was altogether Christ Himself. This point must be made very clear.

The cross works on us to deal exactly with this matter; it breaks us and kills us in order to deal with this very issue. It deals with our own wisdom and overthrows our capable person. Why? Because if our cleverness, wisdom, and ability are not subdued by the Lord, what we do will definitely be of ourselves, not of the Lord. For example, if God had used Moses at age forty to save Israel, his service would have been full of his own ability, cleverness, wisdom, and knowledge. Therefore, God allowed him to run up against a wall. That was the cross breaking his talent, ability, wisdom, and cleverness. He was a prince in the palace and a captain in the army. Yet he was dealt with and became a wanderer and a shepherd in the wilderness. God used all these experiences to break him.

We must see that when we serve in the church and participate in the Lord's work, we absolutely cannot minister what we have in ourselves. Whenever we mix what we have into the Lord's service, the cross will come to us. This is very difficult, because God wants us for His work, but He does not want what we have.

Let us look at the other side of this matter. Although the Lord does not want what we have, He wants us to be useful to Him. After much consideration before the Lord, I believe that the matter of being "useful to the master" has much to do with a man's character. Our talent and ability must not be mixed into the service of the Lord. However, our character can determine whether we are suitable for the Lord's use. The character of some people is useful to the Lord, but that of others is not. Even though those who serve the Lord must not bring in what they have, their character must be suitable for the Lord's use. For this reason, I have been repeating that to be useful to the Master, we must build up a character that is useful to Him. Brothers and sisters, we bear a tremendous responsibility in this matter.

FOUR ASPECTS OF BEING USEFUL TO THE MASTER

What kind of person is useful to the Lord? There are at least four aspects. First, he must love and desire the Lord. Do not even talk about being used by the Lord if you do not love and desire Him. We do not need to cover this basic matter here. Second, he must have a vision of the Lord and an encounter with Him. He needs to have a revelation that God's eternal purpose is to work Christ into us and to express Christ through us. This is a great point. I have met many saints who love the Lord but have not seen this Christ of God. They have seen only Jesus their Savior, not the Christ of God. These may be zealous and full of love, yet in their service they do not minister the Lord to others, because they have not seen this Christ and have not received this revelation. In order to be useful in the Lord's hand, one must see the revelation concerning Christ. Third, his self, his person, must have been dealt with by the cross. He must realize that whatever he has and whatever comes out of him cannot be brought into the Lord's service. His natural being must have been terminated on the cross. Only those who have seen their flesh and their natural man realize how precious the cross is. Only when you have seen that you are fleshly and nothing but a thornbush, a leper, and a natural man will you treasure the experience of the cross. This can be called the revelation of the natural man or the revelation of the cross. After you have a heart to love the Lord, you must have at least two revelations, one concerning Christ and the other concerning the self, which also concerns the cross. You cannot lack any of these three aspects.

However, these three aspects are not sufficient. With these you can do something valuable, but nothing extensive. You will surely dispense Christ and minister Christ, though perhaps only once a year, or to one person in six months.

Suppose there is a brother who sincerely loves the Lord and is not occupied with the world. He has been enlightened, he has seen the Christ of God, and he sees that the purpose of God in this universe is Christ, and that it is to work Christ into men and then to work Christ out from within men. He truly has the revelation of Christ. He also sees that what hinders Christ the most is his self, his flesh, and his natural life, and seeing this, he has fallen down. He has the knowledge of his natural life, which is the revelation of the cross. When you meet this one, you always sense that the Lord is so sweet, so lovely, and so great. However, you see some peculiarity in this brother. For example, if you ask him if he could find time to assist certain brothers who need help, he will answer, "Fine, fine." But when he goes home, he will soon forget about it. Such a thing actually happened. This brother really loves the Lord, receives mercy, and sees himself and the way of the cross; however, there is something lacking in him which renders him useless to the Master.

Later, the same one may become an elder. A brother may come to him saying, "A certain sister has a serious problem related to marriage. She was engaged to someone, but now she is engaged to someone else. What do you think we should do?" He may say, "Well, let us look to the Lord." Then another brother may come, saying, "A certain brother's family is having a difficult time; he lost his job. What should we do?" To this he may reply, "Well, let us pray. If the Lord does not do anything, what can we do?" Do not think that such brothers do not exist. I am afraid to handle business with such brothers and sisters. When I do, I inevitably become frustrated. What is the problem with them? Are they short of love towards the Lord, or do they lack the knowledge of Christ? Or is it that they do not sufficiently know the cross? It is none of these; the problem is entirely with their character.

In all these years we have been studying the matter of service. Through our continuous probing and research, we have reached the conclusion that all of the above four aspects are indispensable. Surprisingly, however, the fourth aspect, the aspect of character, is often easily rejected or neglected. Many assume that as long as they love the Lord, see Christ, and know the way of the cross, they have reached the peak. However, the fact remains that the first three aspects are inadequate. A cook must take four steps to prepare a meal: first, he must go shopping at the market; second, he has to remove many things, such as leaves of bamboo shoots, fish scales, and vegetable roots; third, he needs to cook the food; and fourth, he must prepare the chairs, plates, chopsticks, and spoons. Why is this fourth step necessary? Is the cook serving chopsticks and the table as food? Certainly not. However, without chopsticks, spoons, plates, and a table, the dinner cannot be properly served. These eating utensils illustrate the character of us who serve the Lord. Without them the food will stay in the cookware. One could still eat it but would not enjoy it. No one would eat the chopsticks and spoons along with the food; that would be terrible. We serve people a meal, so that they may eat the food and not the utensils. Similarly, we do not minister our character to others, but we bear Christ to them by our character.

For example, a certain brother may be absent-minded and forgetful. Can his forgetful character replace the Christ whom he knows inwardly? Not at all. But his character greatly affects his service. He must make up this lack if he wants to be suitable for the Lord's use. He must learn to remember things. He should carry a pocket notebook to record things that need to be done. This is just a small example.

THE CHARACTER OF THE LORD'S SERVANTS
IN THE OLD AND NEW TESTAMENTS

Let us now consider the character of those who served the Lord in both the Old and New Testaments. It would actually be very worthwhile for you to study the character of persons from Abraham in the Old Testament to John in the New Testament. We can select only a few of those individuals for our discussion here.

Moses' character was nearly perfect, as we see in the Old Testament. First, he received the knowledge of God from his parents when he was young. This is a factor that contributed to the development of his character. Second, God prepared an environment, bringing him to the Egyptian palace to learn the culture of that age. This also was a factor in the cultivation of his character. Third, God sent him to the wilderness for forty years for character training. Once a prince in the Egyptian palace, he now shepherded a flock, learning patience and humility and spontaneously acquiring a lowly character. For forty years, in the freezing cold and the scorching heat, he took care of his sheep. The ordeals and suffering that he went through were all for the development of his character, to make him humble, accommodating, enduring, patient, and sensitive.

Furthermore, a shepherd must have a sense of responsibility and a caring heart; he must be fine and thorough. A shepherd must lead his flock according to the sheep's need to drink, to graze, to rest, and to move. Later, because of his forty years of training in the wilderness, Moses was able to lead the Israelites for forty years. He learned his lessons for forty years, so he was able to lead for forty years. This shows us that the extent to which God could use him depended on how much his character had been developed before the Lord. There is no doubt that the God who filled Moses was unlimited; however, Moses' ability to testify and minister the God who filled him was based upon the character he had developed during his shepherding years.

It is clear that later, when Moses became God's greatest servant, his character was very strong and capable, as well as fine, thorough, and sympathetic. The law of Moses is very high and very detailed. When he spoke of offerings, he even gave instructions for handling dung. He discussed very thoroughly the way to deal with the problems a woman might face before she is engaged, after she is engaged but before she is married, and after she is married. When you read Moses' Pentateuch again, notice that his character was strong and transparent; at the same time it was also fine, thorough, and accommodating. This is the reason that the fire of Jehovah could burn and be manifested upon him.

In Deuteronomy he recounted events from the time the Israelites received the law until his dying days. How detailed was his memory! His compassion toward the Israelites was many times deeper than a mother's. With such a character it was no wonder that God's fire could burn upon him. Did all this pertain to Moses' spiritual life? Those who do not know God may say so; actually, it was a matter of his character. Since God was manifested through him, God must have been the life, but Moses needed such a character to uphold God's manifestation.

I mention this repeatedly because through the ages those who serve the Lord have neglected the matter of character. Rising early in the morning is not an aspect of the spiritual life; neither is remembering what people entrusted to you. These are matters of character. The spiritual life is the Christ constituted in you, the Christ seen by you, the Christ known by you, the Christ with whom you are filled. The point here is that as Christ has been seen by you and is being ministered to others through you, what kind of character should you have in order to be useful?

Now we come to Paul in the New Testament. Do you not sense that you touch a special character in Paul's fourteen Epistles? Do you not sense here a man who is tender, helpful, accommodating, and frank? He was full of Christ, and the fire of Christ was burning within him and upon him. However, what people sensed was a diligent character, a mind to work, a readiness to speak frankly, a care for others, and a willingness to accommodate others. These points of character constitute the person of Paul. At times he could be extremely severe. Once he asked, "Shall I come to you with a rod, or in

love and a spirit of meekness?" (1 Cor. 4:21). At other times he
was full of gentleness. He also asked, "Who is weak, and I am
not weak? Who is stumbled, and I do not burn?" (2 Cor. 11:29).
What a responsible and conscientious person he was!

SHORTCOMINGS IN OUR CHARACTER

Now let us come back to consider ourselves. I have mentioned that laziness is a major shortcoming in our character.
Especially with regard to the young brothers and sisters, if
you do not build up a diligent character, your work will have
no future. At most you can be only a pretty flower for people
to admire; you can hardly be a vessel to supply God's children.
Even though you may know the cross, Christ, and the natural
man, if you are not diligent enough, it will be difficult for you
to minister Christ to others. Christ will be nullified by your
laziness. If you do not believe my word now, you will twenty
years from now. You do not know how many things you will
spoil because of a lack of diligence in your character.

Many people are willing to take on grand tasks but not
small ones. This also is a shortcoming in character. If you
desire to do only the big things and not the trivial, you are
through. Whoever is useful in the hands of the Lord must be
utterly broad on one hand, and extremely fine on the other.
Such was Moses' law. You should do minor jobs well, and you
should also be able to carry out major assignments. Your
character needs to be dealt with on this point. If you take
pleasure only in preaching the all-inclusive Christ and His
all-inclusive death on the cross, yet you are not willing to
engage in trivial duties in your daily life, there is a shortage
in your character.

Then, there are those people who are careless in everything; this characteristic makes them unsuitable for God's
use. You should be accommodating to others, but you should
not tolerate sloppiness. If you gave a poor message last
night, you cannot excuse yourself and let it go carelessly. You
should condemn yourself, realizing that it was not acceptable.
This may be called a progressive attitude. Some people do not
have this item in their character and are thus of no use to the
Lord.

Some people are irresponsible. Moreover, their irresponsibility is spontaneous and not intentional. If you ask one of them to be an elder, he may agree, albeit with a shallow sense of responsibility. He would not put upon his shoulders the people, things, or matters of the church. It seems that whatever matter you entrust to him becomes lost or disappears. He takes care only of those things which he happens to come across. This is because he lacks a sense of responsibility. The unconscientious person who serves the Lord cannot expect to be able to render help to others. We should not only love and care for people but also learn and practice before the Lord to be conscientious. Once certain matters of the church are entrusted to us, our heart should be in them. We should carry on our heart those whom we prayed for. Learn to have a sense of responsibility.

There is no need to illustrate further. If you check with yourself, you will see that there are still many areas of your character which are unfit for the Lord. As one who lacks the many qualities which are useful to the Lord, you must spend sufficient time to exercise to build up your character. Only then will you be useful to Him.

Never think that it is easier to oversee the church, to preach the gospel, or to save people's souls than to do worldly business. This is absolutely not true. When I was first saved, although I had not yet received the Lord's calling, by His grace I already enjoyed Bible reading, going to meetings, and, at times, gospel preaching. I met a classmate who had lost his job because of his temperament and personality. He came to see me and said, "You are associated with a certain denomination; now that I have lost my job, would you please recommend me to them as a preacher?" When I heard this, I was speechless. Today the common assumption is that it is easier to preach the gospel and serve the church than to do anything else; it seems that there is no need for a proper character and that such work can be done in a heedless way. I was told that anyone who has been a preacher for three years is not able to do anything else. We should feel shameful about these things.

We must realize that for serving the Lord, preaching the

gospel, overseeing the church, and saving souls, a proper human character is the topmost requirement. To do these things, more than any other kind of work, requires diligence, earnestness, endurance, boldness, self-sacrifice, self-denial, thoughtfulness, considerateness, and progressiveness with daily improvement. If these qualities are not in your character, it makes little difference whether you are available for the Lord's service or not.

Therefore, in order to serve the Lord, to preach the gospel, and to establish churches, you must build up a character that is useful to the Lord. In your daily life you need to attend to and diligently learn everything related to character, whether it is great or small. You should not place your clothes or books sloppily; all your belongings must be put in their proper place. This will help you to build up an exact character so that you will not do things in an unclear and careless way. You need to practice to be exact, never speaking carelessly or inaccurately, even remembering precisely the words of the Bible and their references. You need to cultivate your sense of responsibility and to work it into your character. Then, when you administrate the church, you will do nothing carelessly, since a certain conscientiousness will already be in you. May the Lord have mercy upon us that we may realize what kind of character is useful to Him.

CHAPTER SIX

THE OVERTHROWING OF DISPOSITION
FOR THE MANIFESTING OF FUNCTION

Scripture Reading: 2 Cor. 3:18; 4:16

MANIFESTING FUNCTION
BY OVERTHROWING DISPOSITION

In this chapter we will consider the relationship between disposition and function. The matter of disposition is a serious problem among us. I am sure that we have all seen the Lord's way clearly and that our motives are pure. We will take this way even if it means that we must die, laying down our own lives. Still, according to my observation, there is a big problem among us—our disposition, our nature. We are surely destined to take this way, but the extent to which the Lord can have His way in us depends on how much our disposition has been overthrown and our nature broken. The extent to which our disposition has been overthrown determines how much our function will be manifested. I am very clear that the basic hindrance to the manifestation of your function is an unbroken disposition. You all have heard messages on being broken and are clear about them, but you have hardly been broken.

For example, some of the brothers and sisters have a disposition that cannot get along with others. They do not oppose or harass others, nor do they have the intention to disturb anyone. But their disposition prevents them from mingling with others. They would say, "Either I do it and do it all, or you do it and do it completely. It is your responsibility if you fail, and it is my misfortune if I fail." There are many like this today. Such an inborn nature is a very serious problem in the Lord's work. We must realize that the basis of the Lord's work is the principle of the Body. How can we not coordinate together? Some brothers comment that it is very difficult to serve in coordination in the church in Taipei because so many older sisters interfere. There is some truth to this. If you come to Taipei to serve, you have elders above, group leaders below, and ones responsible for the meeting hall in the middle; you will probably be pressed and squeezed from all sides. It is no wonder that many feel as if they cannot continue their service in Taipei. This is a case of disposition. If your disposition has not been dealt with, you can never coordinate with others.

One kind of person is naturally timid. According to the grace and gift he has received, a certain ministry should have been manifested in him. Whereas he could actually bear a load of a thousand pounds, he would bear only twenty. His nature is like a sensitive plant, always shrinking back, always withdrawing, and his usefulness thus comes to a standstill. Another kind of person dares to tackle anything. He accepts whatever is entrusted to him. Even if he is given the earth and the moon, he is not afraid. In the end, since he is actually limited in his ability, rather than accomplishing the work, he spoils it.

DISPOSITION AND NATIONAL CHARACTER

The problems of disposition must be ascribed to our national character. A nation's character deeply affects its people's disposition. Take the Japanese as an illustration. Before I went to Japan, I thought that the Japanese were more talented and capable than the Chinese. After I had stayed in Japan for a period of time and had had some contact with the Japanese, I found that the Japanese cannot compete with the Chinese in terms of intelligence and talent. Their thinking is slow, and they are not very smart or clever. What makes them successful is described in a Chinese proverb: "Diligence can compensate for dullness." The same chore that a Chinese can finish in an hour will take a Japanese at least three hours. I watched children study in the United States. Chinese students need only one hour to study in the evening, while Japanese children need five hours. Chinese children seem to be speed readers; they study their material once and then try their luck on the test the next day. Japanese children are different. The day before the test they painstakingly memorize the material and study until three o'clock in the morning. They can recite every word of the material to be tested, not leaving anything to chance. When a Chinese child takes a test, he finishes it quickly and receives an "A" by chance. A Japanese child reads the questions and answers them scrupulously. He may be very slow, but in the end he also receives an "A." His "A" is sure, whereas the "A" the Chinese child receives is by chance. When chance is not in favor of the Chinese child, he achieves only a "B."

The Japanese are by nature patient and motivated to learn. Whenever I shopped in a Japanese department store, I never had the patience to wait for the salespersons to wrap the merchandise. Invariably, they always continued to say "thank you" while they wrapped. A single package might have been wrapped with three or four layers of paper. Whereas it took me only five minutes to purchase an item, the wrapping took ten. They nodded and bowed with tremendous patience. Everyone knows that the Japanese are not inventive, yet they are diligent to learn; eventually, their imitation is better than your invention.

Though the Chinese are smart and capable, our national character is marked by an ability to do things hastily and skimpily. Today the situation in Taiwan may have improved. Generally, however, the Chinese begin a job well but often conclude it in a sloppy way. Years ago, the fine silk produced in Shantung initially weighed thirty-eight ounces a roll. Gradually, the amount of silk was reduced and was later mixed with starch. In time, the roll contained only twelve ounces of silk, and the quality was lowered to such an extent that the people did not want it anymore. To do things hastily means to finish a task sloppily in three days when normally it would take a week to complete. The Japanese are not like this. They would labor ten days to finish a job that requires only a week to complete, working until the result is perfect. Their national character is truly impressive.

What about the Americans? They are also serious about their work. Either they do a job seriously, or they do not do it at all. They do not treat any work as a side job. Therefore, it is hard for an American to change direction. Once he starts a job according to your instructions, it is almost impossible for him to change. If you tell him to shift direction, he will be very bothered and say, "You have just told me to go south. Why are you telling me to go north?" In dealing with Americans, you must know where you are going; making a change midway inevitably spells trouble, since they will do the wrong thing. On the other hand, if a Chinese is working for you, you can afford to change twenty-eight times. The Chinese are really capable in this regard; no matter how you want to change, they will understand even before you make yourself clear. This is the talent of the Chinese, but in the end the result is seldom satisfactory.

The meeting hall of the church in Los Angeles is cleaned every Saturday. The saints do not come in a sloppy way; they put on work clothes and work seriously. This earnestness is the reason for their success. They are responsible; they do not fool around. They either do something thoroughly, or they do not do it at all. As to the Chinese, we are mostly noncommittal and not absolute.

NOT LIMITED BY DISPOSITION IN THE LORD'S WORK

In principle, our faithfulness and diligence in serving the Lord should exceed our faithfulness and diligence in other business. Since we have consecrated ourselves to the Lord and have given up our future and everything to serve Him, we should be very useful. Unfortunately, we are extremely limited by our disposition and, as a result, too little of our function is manifested. If we do not overthrow our old disposition, I am afraid that our usefulness in the hand of the Lord will cease.

The disposition of some brothers reflects a strong self-confidence. They believe they can do anything and are thus blinded by their self-confidence. After working in one place a year or two, they may have accomplished nothing. Then they may move to another place and still produce no result. However, they always feel that this is because of others' shortage and never their own. Your self-confidence must be over-thrown; do not be self-confident any longer. You will be useful only if such confidence is overthrown. It is primarily due to dispositional limitations that the usefulness of our co-work-ers cannot be fully developed. I am absolutely convinced that if we can break through the constraints of our disposition, the effectiveness of our work will more than triple.

Some people do not know to utilize their environment; rather, they expect their environment to suit them. They refuse to work as long as the circumstances are not perfect or the conditions are not adequate. You must realize that in our work it is almost impossible to have a perfect environment, because we have no organization. How can we expect perfect conditions when practically we are always in need? In mili-tary terms, we are rarely engaged in conventional battles but in guerilla warfare. We have no regular army, only guerilla troops. It all depends on how flexible we are to adapt to our circumstances and adjust to all environments.

When we began the publication work in Taiwan, I wrote articles on a small coffee table at home. I wrote whether there was a desk or not. Do not say that you cannot write or publish without a desk. Whether you have a desk or not, work can still be done. This must be our disposition. Reject the disposi-tion that requires a particular environment before you can work.

We must bring ourselves to a point that we can work in any environment. However, it is useless to learn merely an outward method; we must overthrow our inward disposition. Remember that the degree to which our function will be man-ifested depends mostly on our disposition. If we overthrow our disposition, our usefulness and the fruit of our work will immediately multiply. We all are limited by our disposition. Many problems today are in fact due to our disposition. I cer-tainly hope that the co-workers will be deeply touched by this matter.

CHAPTER SEVEN

CULTIVATING A CHARACTER TO CONTACT PEOPLE

THE NEED TO DEAL WITH OUR CHARACTER

A person's work or service is absolutely related to his character. As his character is, so will be his way of doing things and his work. Many difficulties which we have as serving ones stem from our character. Of course, some of our problems are spiritual and some are emotional. Most problems, however, are caused by our character. Therefore, while learning to serve the Lord, we need to be in constant fellowship with Him and rely on His grace; on the other hand, we also must deal severely with our character.

We ourselves bear the responsibility for dealing with our own character. It seems that it is not easy for the Holy Spirit to do this for us. We cannot say that the Holy Spirit does not touch or interfere with the matters of our character, such as the way we conduct ourselves and the way we do things, but we are wrong if we expect the Holy Spirit to build a good character for us. The Holy Spirit does not do much in this area. Even when He does, He needs our full cooperation.

Some brothers have problems with their character. They never finish thoroughly any task which is put into their hands. After all their efforts, a "tail" always remains. This is a problem of character. Some term this a problem of habit, but we do not think that is a fitting description; rather, we like to call it a problem of character.

LOVING TO CONTACT PEOPLE

One who serves the Lord must have a good character that loves to contact people. Some people by nature like to meet others, but this is natural. It is not in resurrection and is therefore useless. In our service we need to be dealt with by God to the extent that we love to contact people. To speak in non-spiritual terms, we need to deal with ourselves, to force ourselves to contact people.

I asked one of the brothers to tell me how many saints have come from overseas to attend this conference, and I asked him whether he had contacted them. He said that he had contacted only two brothers from Hong Kong and another from Indonesia. Moreover, he did not know their names. Do not think that I am too much. This is where our problem lies. I believe that this brother will allow me to say that to contact people is not an easy thing. This is a problem not only with him but with all of us. As we are here in this training, many young brothers who are serving the Lord are eating in the same dining room and are being trained in the same classroom. The brothers from overseas have come not only to listen to some messages but also to seek fellowship. As a rule, we all should sense a responsibility to fellowship with them and render help to them. Unfortunately, there is a solid wall here which the Spirit can hardly break down. We simply do not have the character to contact people.

Brothers, if we were more broken, or if we had learned more concerning proper spiritual temperament, today we would be receiving even more grace. Among us, grace is not contagious enough, because we are too separated. We should allow grace to infect us, to flow between us to the uttermost. However, according to my observation, there are still many separations among us.

For some brothers and sisters, it is not that they do not like to contact others but that they like to contact only a few special ones. For example, Brother Wu loves to contact Brother Chow, and Brother Chow loves to contact Brother Wu. Brother Chow not only knows Brother Wu's name, but he knows him inside out. There is nothing about Brother Wu that he does not know. However, concerning those from Indonesia, whether their last name is Liu or Wang makes no difference to him. He does not remember clearly how many are here from Manila or from the United States. He does not know which room they are staying in. After staying with them for months, he has not asked their names. How can we serve the Lord with this kind of character?

During the training at Kou Lin in 1948 and 1949, Brother Nee in one lesson told us that in order to be useful in the hand of the Lord, one must be interested in people. One must love to study people and must have an interest in them. In particular, one should always contact the new ones. When such a person helps the new ones, he is happy. He is contented just to talk to them. We must have this kind of temperament; otherwise, our service will be greatly frustrated.

We should come early to every meeting. If the meeting starts at half past seven, we should arrive at seven o'clock. Why should we come early? We should come early to wait for people. It is worthwhile to contact people, even if only for five or ten minutes. Contact them not only before but also after the meeting. If we contact two people before and after every meeting, throughout a week we will have contacted at least ten in five meetings. Perhaps some would say that this is too mechanical. No, if you have this kind of character, you will feel that this is very spontaneous. In every meeting you will contact one when you come and one when you leave. Some say that the saints always leave immediately after the meeting. If this is the case, why not walk with them for some distance? You could walk with them from the meeting hall to the street and exchange a few words with them, asking them about their work and their condition before the Lord. Remember that sometimes just these simple conversations give people great help.

Do not be too official or too formal while contacting people. Do not say, "Now I am serving the Lord, and from three to five in the afternoon every Monday, Wednesday, and Friday I will go out to visit people. My living is regulated and I must wait until three o'clock every Monday, Wednesday, and Friday. I will go out to visit people only after kneeling down to pray for ten minutes." In the end, since no one seems to be home, you return empty. You may then consider this a real discipline of the Holy Spirit, because everyone you wanted to see was not home. Actually, this is a formal, bureaucratic kind of service.

No one would be successful or make a profit in business by using this method. Many times a profitable business deal is consummated on a tennis court over a match or in a coffee shop over coffee.

CONTACTING PEOPLE
AND GIVING GRACE AT ALL TIMES

Brothers, you must learn to have this kind of character; otherwise, believe me, you will be of little use. Our contact with the Lord is one thing, and our contact with people is another. Our contact with the Lord can never replace our contact with people. While He was on the earth, our Lord Jesus always maintained these two kinds of contact. The Lord never went anywhere without contacting people. Everywhere He went, He contacted people. If He did not contact anyone, it was intentional, because of God's will, because He lived under the governing of God's will. He contacted people everywhere. He adapted His messages to changing circumstances, speaking the proper words to each kind of person and for each occasion. His speaking was never monotonous or set, nor was it according to a formula. He was available at all times; therefore, He could give grace at all times and could contact all kinds of people.

Some brothers have the attitude that they have learned the matter of inward fellowship; therefore, they feel that such an activity as contacting people is for those who love excitement, and thus they leave it to others. This concept is wrong. Let me ask you, what lesson did the Lord Jesus learn? Whatever lesson you learn should be in the realm of contacting people. Contact people all the time. When I am with an elderly brother, I learn before him. While meeting young brothers, I render them some help. If there were such a condition in a church, how much blessing there would be! Because of this little practice many people would be brought in, and a fire would be ignited.

Many times after the Lord's table I saw the brothers and sisters leave one by one. This reminds me of the scene in John chapter eight, where the Lord Jesus said, "He who is without sin among you, let him be the first to throw a stone." Hearing these words, the Jews went out one by one, beginning with older ones until the last. It is rare to see two brothers or two sisters talking to each other. Even when people converse, they talk to those with whom they are familiar, and they seldom look for others. This is a most serious problem.

ABOUT THE AUTHOR

Witness Lee was born in 1905 in northern China and raised in a Christian family. At age 19 he was fully captured for Christ and immediately consecrated himself to preach the gospel for the rest of his life. Early in his service, he met Watchman Nee, a renowned preacher, teacher, and writer. Witness Lee labored together with Watchman Nee under his direction. In 1934 Watchman Nee entrusted Witness Lee with the responsibility for his publication operation, called the Shanghai Gospel Bookroom.

Prior to the Communist takeover in 1949, Witness Lee was sent by Watchman Nee and his other co-workers to Taiwan to ensure that the things delivered to them by the Lord would not be lost. Watchman Nee instructed Witness Lee to continue the former's publishing operation abroad as the Taiwan Gospel Bookroom, which has been publicly recognized as the publisher of Watchman Nee's works outside China. Witness Lee's work in Taiwan manifested the Lord's abundant blessing. From a mere 350 believers, newly fled from the mainland, the churches in Taiwan grew to 20,000 in five years.

In 1962 Witness Lee felt led of the Lord to come to the United States, and he began to minister in Los Angeles. During his 35 years of service in the U.S., he ministered in weekly meetings and weekend conferences, delivering several thousand spoken messages. Much of his speaking has since been published as over 400 titles. Many of these have been translated into over fourteen languages. He gave his last public conference in February 1997 at the age of 91.

He leaves behind a prolific presentation of the truth in the Bible. His major work, *Life-study of the Bible,* comprises over 25,000 pages of commentary on every book of the Bible from the perspective of the believers' enjoyment and experience of God's divine life in Christ through the Holy Spirit. Witness Lee was the chief editor of a new translation of the New Testament into Chinese called the Recovery Version and directed the translation of the same into English. The Recovery Version also appears in a number of other languages. He provided an extensive body of footnotes, outlines, and spiritual cross references. A radio broadcast of his messages can be heard on Christian radio stations in the United States. In 1965 Witness Lee founded Living Stream Ministry, a non-profit corporation, located in Anaheim, California, which officially presents his and Watchman Nee's ministry.

Witness Lee's ministry emphasizes the experience of Christ as life and the practical oneness of the believers as the Body of Christ. Stressing the importance of attending to both these matters, he led the churches under his care to grow in Christian life and function. He was unbending in his conviction that God's goal is not narrow sectarianism but the Body of Christ. In time, believers began to meet simply as the church in their localities in response to this conviction. In recent years a number of new churches have been raised up in Russia and in many European countries.

OTHER BOOKS PUBLISHED BY
Living Stream Ministry

Titles by Witness Lee:

Abraham—Called by God	978-0-7363-0359-0
The Experience of Life	978-0-87083-417-2
The Knowledge of Life	978-0-87083-419-6
The Tree of Life	978-0-87083-300-7
The Economy of God	978-0-87083-415-8
The Divine Economy	978-0-87083-268-0
God's New Testament Economy	978-0-87083-199-7
The World Situation and God's Move	978-0-87083-092-1
Christ vs. Religion	978-0-87083-010-5
The All-inclusive Christ	978-0-87083-020-4
Gospel Outlines	978-0-87083-039-6
Character	978-0-87083-322-9
The Secret of Experiencing Christ	978-0-87083-227-7
The Life and Way for the Practice of the Church Life	978-0-87083-785-2
The Basic Revelation in the Holy Scriptures	978-0-87083-105-8
The Crucial Revelation of Life in the Scriptures	978-0-87083-372-4
The Spirit with Our Spirit	978-0-87083-798-2
Christ as the Reality	978-0-87083-047-1
The Central Line of the Divine Revelation	978-0-87083-960-3
The Full Knowledge of the Word of God	978-0-87083-289-5
Watchman Nee—A Seer of the Divine Revelation ...	978-0-87083-625-1

Titles by Watchman Nee:

How to Study the Bible	978-0-7363-0407-8
God's Overcomers	978-0-7363-0433-7
The New Covenant	978-0-7363-0088-9
The Spiritual Man • 3 volumes	978-0-7363-0269-2
Authority and Submission	978-0-7363-0185-5
The Overcoming Life	978-1-57593-817-2
The Glorious Church	978-0-87083-745-6
The Prayer Ministry of the Church	978-0-87083-860-6
The Breaking of the Outer Man and the Release ...	978-1-57593-955-1
The Mystery of Christ	978-1-57593-954-4
The God of Abraham, Isaac, and Jacob	978-0-87083-932-0
The Song of Songs	978-0-87083-872-9
The Gospel of God • 2 volumes	978-1-57593-953-7
The Normal Christian Church Life	978-0-87083-027-3
The Character of the Lord's Worker	978-1-57593-322-1
The Normal Christian Faith	978-0-87083-748-7
Watchman Nee's Testimony	978-0-87083-051-8

Available at
Christian bookstores, or contact Living Stream Ministry
2431 W. La Palma Ave. • Anaheim, CA 92801
1-800-549-5164 • www.livingstream.com